THOMASSON-GRANT & LICKLE

NEW YORK • CHARLOTTESVILLE

KEEPERS OF THE KINGDOM
THE NEW AMERICAN ZOO

PHOTOGRAPHS AND INTRODUCTION BY MICHAEL NICHOLS

ESSAYS BY JON CHARLES COE, WILLIAM CONWAY, DAVID HANCOCKS,

JACK HANNA, EDWARD J. MARUSKA, AND MICHAEL H. ROBINSON

 This new African exhibit at the Pittsburgh Zoo is a testimony to the art of illusion in advanced zoo design. The moat in the foreground simulates a water hole while concealing an underwater fence to prevent free-ranging animals from escaping. The giraffe seen in the distance actually occupies a separate exhibit. Pittsburgh, once considered to be among America's worst zoos, has transformed itself dramatically due to innovative exhibitions like this one.

CONTENTS

A captive-born giraffe *(Giraffa camelopardalis reticulata)* at San Diego's Wild Animal Park, where 325 species of birds and 125 species of mammals live in simulated savanna environments. San Diego pioneered the idea of open enclosures in zoos, with visitors touring habitats by monorail or flatbed truck. San Diego's generous 2,000-acre expanse has permitted the zoo to undertake large-scale husbandry of endangered species, particularly ungulates.

A caress brushes the fifty-five-foot glass window at the Toledo Zoo's popular Hippoquarium, as a child follows Cupid the hippo's balletic underwater bottom-walk. The emphasis on the sight and smell of real animals living in conditions close to the wild marks the new commitment of zoological parks to responsible education.

INTRODUCTION

MICHAEL NICHOLS

"His breath would wilt flowers," photographer Nick Nichols observes, gingerly embracing E.T. the walrus after the big mammal's daily meal of eight pounds of fish at Point Defiance Zoo, Tacoma, Washington.

Recently, with the success of the movie *The Lion King,* I wondered if my culture's view of wildlife was not entirely shaped by such animation. With the best of intentions, we want wildlife to be what we have conditioned ourselves to expect: characters in a cartoon world controlled and determined by human nature. Having worked so much with wild and captive apes, I have seen how frequently our paternal urge to embrace these creatures as cuddly teddy bears is operative. The cry of dismay—"How can they do that—I thought they were vegetarians!"—elicited when an audience sees my photographs of chimpanzees aggressively eating a cooperatively caught monkey only emphasizes that we just cannot accept the truth about the animal kingdom.

Part of the reason for this is that wildlife, as most Americans experience it, is a remote concept. And its reality generally is translated to us through the medium of that ubiquitous institution, the zoo.

Among the highlights of my childhood were those special visits to the Memphis Zoo, a three-hour drive from my hometown in Alabama. Drawn by the lions' roars, we made sure to be at the cat house when the animals were fed huge slabs of meat. The big cats showed excited aggression at this time—only to be found sleeping at all other times. We would stand and watch for hours on end, fascinated equally by their ferocity and their impotence.

Thirty years later, through the looking glass. . . . It was Sunday in Toledo on the frigid shores of Lake Erie. Research had highlighted the state-of-the-art Hippoquarium there as a worthy exhibit. My previous experience with hippos at zoos was singularly unimpressive. They

Opening day at Henry Doorly Zoo, Omaha, whose Lied Jungle is the largest tropical rain forest exhibit in a North American zoo. Replicating three major rain forest environments, of Asia, Africa, and South America, this million-dollar immersion exhibit allows visitors to feel the jungle humidity, hear the sounds of water, the calls of birds, and the growls of a leopard.

always appeared as huge shapes submerged in dark water clouded with their own excrement. Most often, the bored audience would walk up to them, pause for a matter of seconds, and leave. So I was not prepared for the cult following that the hippos Cupid and Bubbles inspired at Toledo. All day the underwater viewing area was full (to the point of claustrophobia) with people waiting for a space to open in the throng in order to share the view. The two hippos seemed to respond to the attention. They swam, or rather walked, underwater along the glass, repeating again and again a loop that gave the audience that "here-they-come-again" thrill. The children followed along the glass with the hippos. (The adults seemed reluctant to show publicly that they too were seduced.) The eyes of the hippos were watching as they made each pass; squeals of delight rang out.

Hippos are not high on the charisma list. They aren't gorillas, or elephants, or even great white sharks. But in a well-thought-out exhibit they become mesmerizing. In the wild, hippos like to defecate in the same spot. At Toledo, that spot is against the viewing glass. Squeals came once again as the hippos whisked their tails furiously when they pooped.

When *National Geographic* asked me to undertake a photographic survey of where the American zoo is today, I had just finished a ten-year journey through the world of great apes, both in the wild and in captivity. My immersion in this subject was total and my sense of its importance as an issue was profound, a reality check on where our closest relatives had evolved to, and a confirmation of the fact that we were pushing them toward extinction.

My response to the zoo proposal, then, was that zoos were not important enough to warrant a similar expenditure of time and energy. Photographers, as a species, have a short life span and consequently must choose their projects with care. Furthermore, *National Geographic* projects, unlike those of other magazines, tend to make a lengthy and lasting impression on one's body of work.

My hesitation came from my decades-old memory of zoos: zoos as places of depression, bastions of captivity, filled with bored, lifeless animals that might just as well have been stuffed. Having become such an advocate of wilderness protection, I asked myself whether it was worth searching for what was good about zoos. Zeroing in on what was wrong with zoos seemed just too easy.

But I decided that a break from the tropical rain forests of the world and all the wonderful diseases that you enjoy if you frequent them was in order. I could be at home more and watch my kids grow gradually, instead of in gigantic spurts. That assessment was eighteen hundred rolls of film ago. Once I started I became obsessed with finding the best that zoos had to offer. It didn't prove as hard as I thought, because zoos, too, are obsessed with

keeping up with the Joneses. In fact, it is the zoos-as-Chamber-of-Commerce-gadgets approach ("if Pittsburgh has it, Philadelphia must, too") that gets these institutions into trouble. Too many cities try to live above their means by having a zoo they can't afford.

What I found out on my journey is that zoos in general are doing a very good job of policing themselves. At Omaha's Henry Doorly Zoo, I was on hand for opening day at their ambitious Lied Jungle. The dream of director Lee Simmons ("Doc" as he is affectionately called by his very close-knit staff), the exhibit marks the evolution of a trend started by William Conway at the Bronx Zoo's JungleWorld. It is one of the leading ecosystem-style exhibits that point out the intricacies of nature, bringing special attention to the interconnectedness of all the world's most threatened and precious resources, and highlighting the message that they could well be destroyed before we understand what we have lost.

To recreate a rain forest in the middle of America's prairie is no mean feat. Plants must survive in spite of the lack of light for the winter months. Nondangerous mammals and reptiles are free to roam inside a building that resembles a scaled-down Superbowl. Birds and bats are allowed to fly and roost wherever they choose. Heating and cooling costs must be a significant concern, especially since Omaha is hardly a wealthy megacity zoo. Behind the scenes is a computer-driven system that controls lights, air movement, humidity, watering systems, and a myriad of other details. The extraordinary technological achievement that zookeeping today represents is one of its least understood, and therefore unheralded, accomplishments. These expensive replications of nature seduce visitors and then educate them about the benefits of preserving habitats rather than species alone. Critics of such extravagance ask if the animals are truly better off in the fancy (but still false) environments.

Orangutans are very intelligent, able to find and exploit the fruit trees in their wild habitat. In zoos they are supplied with food and no zoo exhibit yet offers the vertical challenge of their natural world. The National Zoo's Orangutan Transit System, tested in 1995, allows the apes to leave their night quarters, go to an exercise yard, climb a tower, and brachiate (swing by their arms) across cables thirty-five feet above the zoo grounds to several other towers (where electric barriers prevent the orangs from descending to the ground) from which they can reach an enclosure called the "Think Tank" (an exhibit on animal intelligence in the historic former monkey house). The tests have highlighted some serious dilemmas. While several orangs made the journey across, one maturing young male ignored the shocks, climbed down a tower, and had to be anesthetized. This heightened the government-owned zoo bureaucracy's greatest fear: the specter, à la Jurassic Park, of extremely strong orangs loose in Washington. The proponents of the exhibit worry that another incident might doom the process. It would be a shame if such forward thinking doesn't reach fruition, as the concept enables the public to witness a true approximation of this animal's exceptional ability. The orangutan's intelligence does make escape-proofing a difficult task, but such bold, ambitious attempts to provide a unique environment for them must be encouraged throughout the zoo world.

Meanwhile, man is trying to fight the tide of extinction by playing God—creating designer condors, ferrets, tigers, panthers, and other endangered animals. This conjures up visions of Frankenstein and other imaginative scenarios that may someday not be out of the question. Moral issues aside, do we stand by and witness extinctions? Or do we do something to preserve that little piece of the wild that we are managing to hold on to? Zoos, those places of Sunday entertainment, are now positioned to respond to those weighty issues, to become the captains of the ark. We have arrived at a time and place where those questions

Near these Malayan tapirs *(Tapirus indicus)* in the Asian rain forest section of JungleWorld at New York's Bronx Zoo are silvered-leaf monkeys, white-cheeked gibbons, black leopards, and more. This pioneering exhibit also includes a rich range of botanical specimens, including mangroves, orchids, ferns, mosses, shrubs, and thirty species of tropical trees.

Twilight silhouettes a rare northern white rhinoceros *(Ceratotherium simum cottoni)* at the San Diego Wild Animal Park. Only forty exist worldwide; half of them live in captivity, and another twenty live wild at Garamba National Park in Zaire.

An unusual white alligator *(Alligator mississippiensis)*, one of eighteen male alligators hatched together, floats in "suspended animation" at the Audubon Zoo's Louisiana Swamp exhibit. Combining flora and fauna as well as information about the history and folklore of marshlands people, this is one of the first exhibits in America to join sociological and cultural elements. Nutria, cougars, black bears, otters, opossums, raccoons. rabbits, alligators, gars, woodcocks, and egrets all live in the exhibit, alongside palmettos, Louisiana irises, maples, sycamores, hackberries, oaks, and gum trees.

Outside New Orleans' Audubon Zoo a barred owl *(Strix varia)* found ensnared in a fishing line is released by Jamie Primm (left), director of the wild bird rehabilitation program, and a park ranger (right). Besides tending their own animals, zoos must cope with migrating birds, vermin, and unwanted pets often left on their doorsteps.

A hunter is employed by Florida Fish and Game to track, tree, and tranquilize a Florida panther, which is then collared by a veterinary team, reexamined, and released back into Big Cypress National Preserve. The Florida panther *(Felis concolor coryi)* is part of a small population of mountain lions also known as cougar, panther, catamount, painter, and, most commonly, mountain lion. The panther is the only great predator that has managed to survive in the eastern United States. Only about thirty remain, and many of them are sterile. The New Opportunities in Animal Health Sciences (NOAH) center at the National Zoo is conducting genetic studies of Florida panthers and is using frozen semen and in vitro fertilization to try to expand their population in the wild.

Roadside menageries like this one in Florida are nonmembers of the zoo club. They are not officially regulated by the American Zoo and Aquarium Association (AZA), but the AZA does monitor complaints against them. Here, a zookeeper teases a captive cat with a shoe in order to create a photo opportunity.

Wild herds of Przewalski's horses *(Equus przewalski)* roamed the Mongolian plains as recently as 1940, but as urban populations expanded, the animal fled to terrain less capable of sustaining it. By the 1960s the horse had vanished, and now survives only in zoos and parks. At a managed breeding program at TheWilds (a reserve in southeastern Ohio established with the cooperation of five zoos), horses run free on reclaimed strip-mining land.

JungleWorld at the Bronx Zoo made history in zoo design and spawned imitators after it was built in 1985. This wood-and-glass-enclosed ecosystem where visitors can be in close proximity to the animals and plant life of a real jungle, complete with mist, trees, vines, and waterfalls, is still both popular and educational.

From Zoos to Conservation Parks

William Conway,
President and General Director,
Wildlife Conservation Society

All over the world, nature and wildlife are being destroyed at an ever faster rate. Zoological parks and aquariums have seemed destined to become no more than living museums of natural history—until recently. Now a developing new synthesis of zoo programming and expertise suggests that the future of zoos is to become "conservation parks" actively contributing to nature's survival—not quiescent museums.

There are at least eleven hundred zoos and aquariums in the world, with a combined annual attendance of about 800 million, a global activity significant both to wildlife and society. But for the vast majority of human beings, the survival of the wildlife they do not eat is irrelevant and doomed to become more so. Saving competitive, possibly dangerous, creatures must seem an unreasonable luxury to the growing ranks of poverty-stricken peoples.

The main problem is human population growth. There are 97 million more of us every year—three every second, about 2.5 billion pounds every twelve months; a proliferation fueling exponential change. In forty years, motor vehicles have increased from 53 million to 500 million. The next few decades can be depended upon to bring national disputes over food, fuel, and water, even if there are new crops and systems that produce more food. There will be disruptive migrations of poorer peoples, even if there are gradual declines in population growth. New diseases will appear, even if new cures are discovered for old ones. Crowding and poverty will stoke tribal warfare, as they have from Afghanistan to Yugoslavia. Thus, society's chances of caring for the earth's surface in ecosystems, rather than habitat fragments, are remote. And the advances humans make in feeding our numbers will subtract from what is left for the rest of life on earth.

William Conway, director of the Wildlife Conservation Society, oversees the five urban zoos in New York City: Bronx Zoo/Wildlife Conservation Park, Aquarium for Wildlife Conservation, and the Queens, Prospect Park, and Central Park wildlife centers, as well as conservation programs in forty-six countries. A distinguished field biologist in his own right, Conway is also a forceful and eloquent advocate of a new ethic for zoos.

An ibex *(Capra ibex nubiana)* and a gelada baboon *(Theropithecus gelada)* share their living space in the new Ethiopian Highlands exhibit in the Bronx Zoo. The variety of species and interaction between animals help relieve the boredom of captivity.

Moreover, nearly 90 percent of human population growth is taking place where the most abundant and fascinating wildlife dwells, in less developed tropical countries. Yet, there are hopeful signs: China, Thailand, Cuba, and Singapore have cut their fertility rates in half, and another fifteen countries have reduced theirs by better than 40 percent.

Accelerated climate change is probably inevitable, however, and its effects upon wild animal communities confined to ever-shrinking fragments of habitat in a swelling sea of humanity will be catastrophic, no matter what its impact is upon humans. Although much marine life is threatened, terrestrial wildlife is almost infinitely more endangered.

Thus, the foreseeable future of the zoo and the wildlife it stands for can be likened to that of a library whose books are decaying and authors dying, a museum whose paintings, artists, and even history are expiring. As species biomass declines, the rare creatures left behind are made obsolescent, not only economically but also ecologically, for they can no longer fulfill their roles in nature. The reasons for preserving or restoring them dwindle to the intellectual ones of curiosity, ethics, and aesthetics—inducements likely to win strongest support in a world free from want.

Our apocalyptic perceptions of the terrestrial extinction crisis are partly drawn from the observation that tropical forest invertebrates are extraordinarily numerous, localized, and diverse. Although there may be more than 30 million species, deforestation is proceeding at the rate of 16 million hectares each year, and we stand to lose hundreds of thousands, perhaps millions, of forms not yet even known. What seems worse is that we shall also lose thousands of larger creatures we do know—members of our phylum.

Extinction forecasts for vertebrates are less dramatic simply because there were few to begin with, but their survival also depends upon available habitat. About 47,500 vertebrate species remain alive, of which 24,500 are sharks and fish and 23,000 are mammals, birds, reptiles, and amphibians. Perhaps 12 percent have representatives in zoos and aquariums. At the least, 25 percent of the tetrapods and 10 percent or more of the fish are

A family of snow monkeys *(Macaca fuscata)* enjoys the cold climate of New York's Central Park Wildlife Center. This urban pocket zoo has chosen to concentrate on a few thoughtfully chosen species, all appropriate to the climate and space available. Tight budgets force many cities to refurbish aging zoos like this, rather than build anew, and Central Park is a model of such renovation.

Largest member of the dog family, the wolf *(Canis lupus)* has an unwarranted reputation for aggression that causes many humans to fear it. Persecuted through much of its North American range, the wolf is still fairly numerous in Canada. This wolf is part of a pack that lives in a large enclosure at the Minnesota Zoo.

A rare Siberian tiger *(Panthera tigris)* plays in the snow at the Minnesota Zoo, where he successfully bred with a female donated from Russia. Minnesota's suitable climate helped in coordinating the breeding program for the American Association of Zoos and Aquariums' Tiger Survival Plan. The original tiger exhibit was so large that visitors complained they could not see the animal—so the size was halved, a compromise that zoos are often pressed to make. This zoo has made headlines for its in vitro fertilization work (with Henry Doorly Zoo and the National Zoo). As a result, there are now twice as many Siberian tigers in captivity as in the wild.

Hippopotamus amphibius is extinct in some of its natural ranges in Africa, but is still relatively numerous elsewhere. Cupid and Bubbles, the resident pair of hippos at the Toledo Zoo, have had eleven offspring.

There is currently a moratorium on elephant breeding in zoos. While the babies are very popular, there are few appropriate exhibit spaces available for them. This baby Asian elephant *(Elephas maximus)* resides at Busch Gardens in Tampa, Florida.

Despite the toothy appearance of its long snout, the gavial *(Gavialis gangeticus)* is harmless to humans. In its natural range in the Ganges and other Indian rivers (where it is seriously endangered) it feeds on fish. These gavials rub noses at JungleWorld at the Bronx Zoo.

The life cycle of the flamboyant flower beetle *(Eudicella gralli)* is described at the Cincinnati Zoo. One of many successfully propagated insects at Cincinnati, the beetle is part of an exhibit that also includes the Hercules beetle, the royal beetle, the Goliath beetle, and the harlequin beetle.

Consisting of a maze of sixty-five displays housing literally millions of living insects, the building covers 7,560 square feet, of which 4,320 square feet constitute the net exhibit area and public space. It has received four Edward Bean Awards for being the first North American zoo to breed and rear in captivity the following: the Goliath beetle, the Giant Southeast Asian walking stick, the Hercules beetle, and the harlequin beetle.

The World of Insects continues to be one of our most popular exhibits. We not only show the insects themselves, but offer information on what insects eat and which predators keep them under control. Not only do we display insects, but we interpret them as well so that they are no longer alien to most people.

The success of the exhibit as a teaching tool can be measured by the fact that there is no biological concept that cannot be dealt with in that one building. One can deal with camouflage, mimicry, and even predation (the necessity of one species preying upon another to keep a healthy balance in an ecosystem). The building is probably the heart of our entire zoo in terms of teaching biological concepts. It has become a model that we have expanded upon and taken into other areas.

And the process continues to yield information. We have discovered that before visitors enter the building, they may not like insects, but if you survey the same visitors again when they leave, they have a better grasp and understanding of insects. Some visitors may not like insects any more than they did when they went in, but now, at least, they understand their importance. We have also learned that young boys and girls relate more to insects and other invertebrates displayed here because of their small size.

There are other animals that need this attention; amphibians are a perfect example. We now recognize that amphibians are possible biological indicators of a healthy or not-so-healthy environment. They are very thin-skinned, live in habitats that border both water and land, and are the first to suffer the full impact of the pollution that threatens all life forms.

Because of acid rain, some species are suffering from changes in the pH of the water in which they breed. They, along with fish, are some of the first in the aquatic realm to experience losses, sometimes from the introduction of alien game fish predators into their breeding ponds, or from excessive ultraviolet rays due to the depletion of the ozone layer.

I first became interested in amphibians more than twenty years ago when most zoos still relegated these animals to small corners of vast reptile collections. When I began to do research into the behavior and husbandry of these animals, little was actually known about them. They are, in fact, extremely fascinating and diverse.

The amphibian population worldwide has been declining at an alarming rate,

During the education program at New Orleans' Audubon Zoo, a keeper shows zoogoers a large poisonous toad *(Bofo marinus)*.

and we have already lost numerous amphibians, particularly frog species. The unsettling thing is that the reasons for these reductions are probably multifaceted. Even amphibians in pristine habitats, for example, can suffer a sudden disappearance. The golden toad in Costa Rica is a prime example. One of the most spectacular amphibians in the world, the golden toad was one of the very few in which the males were a different color than the females. While the females were blotched with a few red markings, the males were a brilliant orange color. The golden toad had a very short breeding period. With the first heavy rains of spring, they would emerge for a few nights for a brief spawning period. Their range was only a few square miles in the Monteverde Cloud Forest Reserve, and it was one of nature's grand phenomena to see many hundreds of these brilliantly colored amphibians in the shallow forest pools. In the early 1980s, there were still hundreds in existence. But researchers found the last of the species in 1989.

The Cincinnati Zoo was the first to breed the Texas blind salamander, and we are hoping to repeat that success with the endangered giant salamanders of Japan and China, both through natural breeding methods and, if necessary, with assisted reproduction techniques.

Center for the Reproduction of Endangered Wildlife (CREW) members at the Cincinnati Zoo collect the eggs of an African eland *(Taurotragus derbianus)*, hoping to freeze the embryo, then transport it to Africa for implanting. Successful embryo transfer begins with the ability to keep eggs, sperm, or embryos alive and healthy outside of their natural environments. CREW researchers have developed techniques to sustain the life of animal reproductive cells and also promote the natural growth of eggs and embryos in vitro. After being collected from an animal and placed in a petri dish, cells continue to grow until they are placed in a surrogate.

One of the major problems faced in the display and breeding of amphibians occurs when you have a hatching with many hundreds of offspring. Logistically, raising all these offspring becomes a nightmare. Our Center for Reproduction of Endangered Wildlife (CREW) is working toward cryogenically freezing fertilized and unfertilized amphibian eggs. It is our hope that the gametes—sperm, eggs, and embryos—can be cryogenically preserved and later transported, thawed, and introduced at the habitat of the endangered species. There is great potential in these methods for future amphibian conservation, because tremendous amounts of genetic material can be stored and later transported to the breeding site without taking up a great deal of room.

The diversity of amphibians is fantastic. Common frogs, toads, and salamanders are ones that everyone recognizes. Some of the tropical forms of amphibians, however, are most bizarre, particularly in terms of their breeding behaviors. The foam-nesting frogs of Africa build their nests in trees above the water. The nest substance hardens, only to soften again when the eggs within begin to hatch, causing the larvae to drop into the water. Other amphibian species carry their eggs on their back. The females of the Surinam toad press their offspring into the males' spongy backs where the developing eggs incubate under the skin until they hatch. There they go through an entire metamorphosis and appear as tiny miniatures of the adults. One species, the marsupial frog, has a pouch on its back to carry its developing eggs.

Other forms are cryptically camouflaged to blend in with their surroundings. There is even one small species which in a resting state resembles a bird dropping, as a means of protection against being preyed upon. The brightly colored poison dart frogs have toxic skin secretions and use their coloration to telegraph their presence to would-be predators. As a form of protection, the shovel-nosed tree frog has a spatula-shaped head that it uses to cover the opening of its burrow so that interlopers cannot enter. The spiny-headed tree frog, meanwhile, has a very thorny head, which may prevent it from being eaten by would-be predators.

Australia's gastric brooding frog, which became extinct in 1980, had one of the most interesting amphibian reproduction behaviors. The tadpoles had to evolve while learning to live with gastric juices because of the frog's habit of brooding its offspring in its stomach and then expelling them as tadpoles or immature frogs.

Amphibians range in size from no larger than a matchstick to some species such as the giant salamander that reach almost five feet in length. They occur in enormous numbers and were the first vertebrates to leave the water and dominate the land. So in an evolutionary sense, they played an important role. Today they are still significant in that they

are the building blocks of many of our ecosystems. You cannot destroy large parts of any ecosystem and not cause a domino effect.

Amphibians are widely scattered all over the world except for the Antarctic, and amphibian populations have experienced serious losses for the past twenty years. As the modern barometer of our environment, warning us to pay more attention to environmental problems, they act as the miner's canary did years ago. The rapid loss of these delicate animals broadcasts problems that will eventually affect other life forms in the environment.

It is our educational task as zoological institutions to explain how nature works and how we are all directly tied to the intricate web of biological diversity. Through our efforts, we must motivate our members, visitors, and the general public to get involved in preserving this diversity. This is not an easy task, but one well worth the effort. Our very existence may depend upon how successfully we accomplish these goals.

Eld's deer *(Cervus eldi thamin)* is an endangered species native to Burmese rain forests. Seven were born from artificial insemination of frozen semen at the Conservation and Research Center (CARE) in Front Royal, Virginia, a research arm of the National Zoo.

The Western tarsier *(Tarsius bancanus)* is also part of the Front Royal program. Tarsiers, native to the jungles of Sumatra and Borneo, have never been successfully bred in captivity, in part because of a lack of knowledge about their diet and habits.

As part of the safari tour at the San Diego Wild Animal Park, visitor Kim Pfiefer feeds a giraffe. With education a large part of most zoo programs, daily shows, interpretive graphics, and a wide variety of both on-site and in-school activities for students are offered, teaching visitors about global and local conservation issues.

69

Cincinnati keeper Mike Dunleavy walks an aardvark *(Orycteropus afer)* around the zoo so that visitors can experience the curious animal's odd appearance and distinctive malodorous scent.

Cathryn Hilker, head trainer of the "cat ambassador program," shows visitors at St. Bernard's Elementary School of Cincinnati a snow leopard *(Panthera uncia)*. For more than twelve years Hilker has regularly visited local schools with cheetahs and other big cats and discussed cat conservation issues.

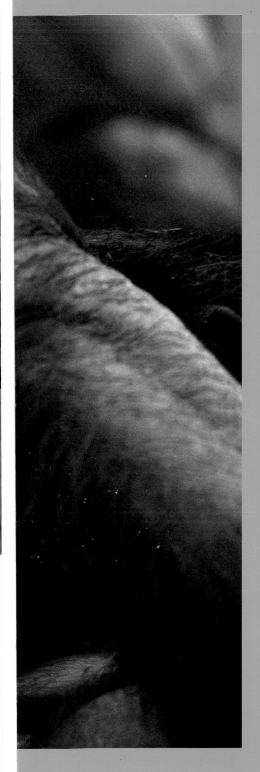

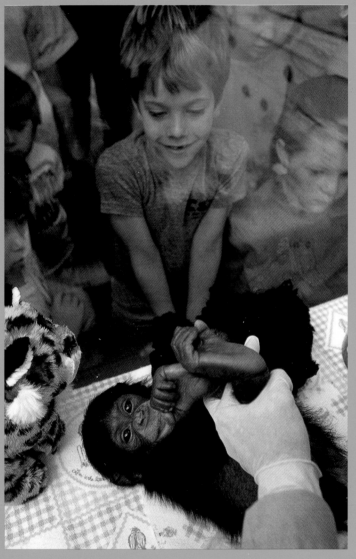

Left: These two bonobos are grooming. In 1994 there were 103 bonobos in captivity worldwide, of which 51 were in North America—a small gene pool that threatens genetic viability. The bonobos in the United States are being managed closely by the Species Survival Plan and have had some reproductive success compared with other great apes. Importing more bonobos from Zaire, their only habitat, is prohibited now under the international CITES treaty and illegal under a poorly enforced Zairean law.

Above: Rejected by its mother, a baby bonobo *(Pan paniscus)* is hand-raised in a nursery in the San Diego Wild Animal Park. San Diego has a program specializing in bonobos, rarest of the great apes.

Cincinnati is one of the last zoos continuing to use animal acts, now seen as a questionable practice for entertaining the public. Like many zoos, it is caught in the dilemma between the need for higher gate receipts and revenues (to cover expensive operating costs), and the obligation to conservation education.

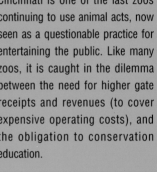

Curator Rick Atkinson feeds the alligators in public at the Louisiana Swamp exhibit of Audubon Zoo, New Orleans, twice weekly, proving to visitors that these somnolent creatures are in fact, alive—and not stuffed!

86

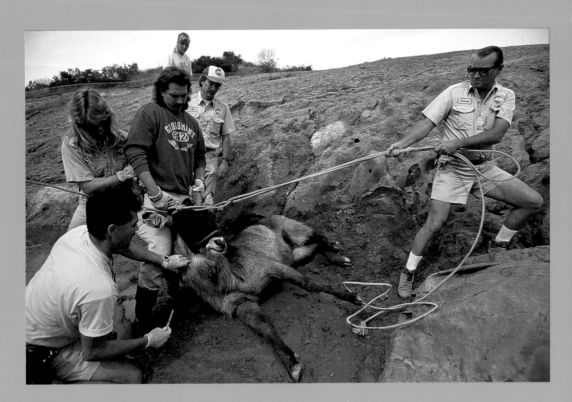

Open spaces create special management problems at zoos. A sick waterbuck at San Diego Wild Animal Park has to be cornered and lassoed by a veterinary team, then anesthetized in order to be taken to the hospital.

Zookeeper Dave Gonzalez gets some help cleaning up the black-and-white colubus monkey
(Colobus guereza kikuyuensis) exhibit at San Diego Wild Animal Park.

This pair of shoebill storks *(Scopus umbreha)* from the savanna swamps of Africa were hand-raised by their African exporter and consequently follow their keeper everywhere (here the male stork performs breeding displays with the keeper, rather than with his mate). The stork's diet consists of lungfish, water snakes, baby turtles, and even crocodiles. Recent numbers in the wild hover at around eleven thousand, but are declining. The shoebill stork has never been bred in captivity and only six exist in U.S. zoos, but zoos such as Chicago's Brookfield Zoo continue to try.

Lowland gorillas *(Gorilla gorilla)* have gentle dispositions and vegetarian habits but are increasingly endangered in their native Africa. Poachers and steady land encroachment by human beings are reducing their numbers; only fifty thousand remain. Meanwhile gorilla exhibits, like other exhibits featuring large, charismatic animals at zoos, are increasing in complexity. Most cost far more than the half a million dollars or so it took to remodel this bear pit at the Woodland Park Zoo in Seattle. Busch Gardens' new gorilla exhibit came to $6 million, and the Bronx Zoo plans a new gorilla enclosure at a conservative estimate of $10 million.

Gardens of Ecology

David Hancocks, Executive Director,
Arizona-Sonora Desert Museum

There have been welcome improvements in many zoos in the past couple of decades, especially in Australasia and North America. Some zoos have created large, densely planted exhibit areas. Zookeepers often engage their creative energy in environmental enrichment techniques that greatly improve the quality of life for the animals in their care. Veterinary health care, hygiene, and nutrition standards have made impressive strides.

All these enhancements, however, have not helped to resolve the fundamental problems. We are faced with an urgent need to do more than just fix and tinker with an outdated concept. It is now time to start planning entirely new types of natural history institutions.

Trying to change tradition is very, very difficult. Zoo collections, for example, have from their beginnings always comprised an inadequate and narrow view of the animal world, focused on charismatic megafauna. I know from personal experience, however, that trying to remove such animals as elephants, jaguars, lions, and polar bears from a zoo collection can generate a lot of political heat and even hate mail from schoolkids. Isn't every zoo expected to have elephants? And giraffes? And zebras, and monkeys, hippos, apes — and lions and tigers and bears? Oh my! The typical zoo collection features but a small and repetitive slice of animal life. Worse, the way these animals are presented in zoos gives no sense of the functional roles they play in their ecosystems.

Until recent times, zoo visitors did not anticipate learning anything but the size, shape, and color of some exotic animal species. That may have been sufficient then; it is not enough for today. There are vital lessons that zoos can give, lessons that our modern world is sorely in need of.

Bighorn sheep *(Ovis canadensis)* at the Arizona-Sonora Desert Museum in Tucson.

We have been engaged in battle with nature ever since we devastated the Pleistocene megafauna in most parts of the world. The conflict accelerated when we started our agricultural revolution. It quite suddenly became more serious, however, about two hundred years ago, with the advent of the industrial revolution. In the past fifty years we have so intensified the rate and scale of destruction that one might be excused for thinking we were officially at war with nature, determined to wipe it out.

Less than twenty generations ago, my ancestors lived in huts of sticks and mud, with no warmth, no ventilation, no light. It is inarguable that we have gained much since then. But the world of those ancestors also gave them daily contact with important things we've lost: a world of birdsong, starry skies, long walks over the hills; intimate contact with little animals in the hedgerows; a detailed consciousness of the way things grow, and of all those subtle complexities of nature that can only be perceived in close and perpetual observation; a world where you took apples from the trees and potatoes from the ground and fish from wild streams. To be aware of these losses is not just nostalgic romanticism. As we have moved to distance ourselves from nature, we have deluded ourselves that we are no longer a part of nature.

We seem now to think we can do what we will and take what we want with impunity. We cover fertile valleys with factories and drain wetlands for malls. We reduce great forests to dust, dam rivers to a standstill, and plough savannas out of existence. We exterminate plants and animals with no knowledge of their medicinal or food potential, no sense of their place in ecology, and we often send them into the abyss of extinction unnamed.

Today, according to Peter Vitousek, an ecologist at Stanford, one animal species, *Homo sapiens*, now uses 40 percent of the terrestrial primary productivity of the planet, and this figure could double in the next thirty years. E. O. Wilson, the Harvard biologist, tells us that we are losing species, principally in the tropical rain forests, at the rate of three an hour. These are statistics beyond comprehension.

Small and specialized areas of the planet give us warning about what is happening. More than half of the different freshwater fish once found in peninsular Malaysia, for example, are gone. All the tree snails on the island of Moorea are gone. Hawaii is on the edge of a precipitous drop in native birds and insects, with a number of plants left without pollinators in the process. Bigger areas are probably responding in the same way, only more slowly. Humanity is facing a calamitous problem.

Zoos have responded to this situation by repeatedly and loudly claiming to be the modern Noah's Ark. This simple imagery no doubt came from the media and publicity departments, rather than the zoologists, but is nonetheless ludicrous. Zoos will save

This exhibit of African elephants *(Laxodonta africanus)* and one Asian elephant *(Elephas maximus)* at Woodland Park, Seattle, winds through the zoo to allow elephants to roam. While a good idea in theory, in practice the exhibit has proved slow to catch on with the elephants, who tend to congregate in the same area. Zoo keepers have discovered that elephants like the stimulation of work (in Thailand they are used as bulldozers) both for exercise and to counter boredom, and some exhibits at new zoos develop tasks like log-moving expressly for animal enrichment.

some species, but these will be the species important to zoos, not necessarily those important to nature.

More than 95 percent of all animals are smaller than a hen's egg and are unknown to zoos. Yet these little animals often have behaviors and lifestyles more interesting and illuminating than typical zoo collections. They are also invariably more critical to the habitat, because they usually have more biomass and thus greater influence, as well as more vital and direct links to the functions of their ecosystems.

It is more than just unfortunate that the little life forms are ignored by zoos. Without them, the interpretations zoos can give about the wild are crippled, and the stories zoos could tell about maintenance and management of habitats are severely compromised. It is the little life forms that run the world.

The loss of even one species of bird or mammal is heartbreaking, but if, say, insects were wiped out (and we seem to be doing our damnedest to insure that), or some other group of tiny organisms, the disruption to the planet's ecosystems would be so massive that it could actually mean the end of almost all other life forms, including humans. Even more likely, the eradication of just a few critical species of pollinating insects would have such an impact on agriculture that it could lead to the collapse of our civilization. It sounds paradoxical, but closer attention by zoos to interpreting the inconspicuous microfauna and their world could help us develop a broader, bigger view of the whole of nature.

Loss of biological diversity is at present recognized as a problem only by scientists. Many of them consider it the greatest of all environmental threats. Sustaining diversity in nature is essential to our own economic, cultural, and psychological well-being, yet it is virtually unknown by the general public. There is much concern about air pollution, oil spills, forest clear-cutting, and thinning of the ozone layer. These environmental issues can make dramatic headlines. They affect us personally. But the insidious loss of biodiversity? How do we relate to that? In a recent poll sponsored by Defenders of Wildlife, not one person in a 1,500-person sample recognized biodiversity loss as a problem. In fact, only one in five Americans says he or she has even heard of it.

Zoos are visited by millions each year. Many come with open minds, hungry for contact with the "other" world of nature. There is enormous potential for zoos to help these visitors understand the richness and complexity of nature. But this potential lies untouched. To reach it, zoos must dramatically broaden their scope. If they do not, they will not only be inadequate for the next century, they will fail, and disappear like dinosaurs.

What evolutionary changes, then, could zoos begin to make? First, it would benefit them greatly to take a very close look at their goals and philosophies, especially by asking themselves the fundamental question: What are zoos for? If their answer emerges, as it well might, "For the breeding of rare and endangered species," I would urge them to repeat the exercise. Surely, if you wanted to create a facility whose central purpose was breeding rare or endangered species, you would not design it to be a public zoo. Zoos are essentially places for exhibition and, consequently, for interpretation. Their very best purpose, and one beyond value, is public education.

If interpretation of nature is the justification for zoos and if the focus of zoological gardens is too narrow to achieve this, then we should expand them in scope and be content to become Gardens of Ecology.

In ecology gardens, visitors could gain strategically important contacts with nature, discover the connections between plants, soils, microorganisms, and characteristic animals within a natural habitat, and thereby learn important new insights. Here they could explore the dynamics of ecosystems. Gardens of Ecology could reveal holistic views of nature. Their visitors would have greater opportunity to develop respect for the astonishingly diverse world of nature, and thereby a new concern for its health and well-being.

In our present system, if you visit a zoo the chances are you will learn nothing about plants; they are typically provided only as a backdrop. A visit to the botanical gardens will just as likely fail to reveal any information about animals. Should you wander through their tropical conservatory you will not see any pollinators. The birds (maybe also a few giant or social insects) are over at the zoological gardens. No one is revealing to the public even such a basic phenomenon as the coevolution of plants and pollinators. How, then, are people to develop an understanding of why such interrelationships are critical?

The tyranny of tradition often prevents us from making changes and may stop zoological parks from expanding their roles. Yet, within their present limits, zoos cannot fulfill their potential. Promoting biological diversity is probably the most important message they can give to their public and the most valuable contribution they can make to conservation.

A shoebill stork at San Diego Wild Animal Park.

They cannot achieve this, however, within the constraints of their present focus.

Coupled with the need for a change in their perspective, zoos must also shift away from exhibiting just individual species; no more "elephant exhibits," "gorilla exhibits," "panda exhibits," or the like. At the same time future zoo plans based on the tidiness of taxonomic groupings must be discarded; no more "feline houses," "bird halls," "reptile pavilions," and so on. Instead, zoos must move toward interpreting *ecosystems*. In trying to do this they will find more intellectually stimulating challenges; greater power and meaning to their mission; and the opportunity to help develop a more fully informed citizenry with a deeper understanding of the natural world.

People of immense vision and optimism created the early zoological gardens. Today's zoo leaders need to emulate that zeal and foresight. Certainly those pioneers would not be grateful for anyone clinging to their old ideas. Worse, neither will unborn generations.

It could not have been easy to establish the new zoological gardens of the 1800s and 1900s. It must, though, have been great fun, and exciting. We can do the same in the 2000s. We can conceive and develop gardens of biology, new institutions that present and interpret natural habitats and their complete biotic communities. We can test our ingenuity and learn how to tell the stories of nature.

Zoos cannot reveal the full story of nature. They restrict themselves to just a small part of the chapter on zoology. That is one good reason they should change their name; the bonds of nomenclature prevent new beginnings, new ways of thinking. Conforming to old ways blocks the opening of new opportunities. The inadequacies of zoos have perpetuated false images in the past, and still convey wrong perspectives for the present generation. Clearly, we are failing to teach even the basics about what our planet is and how it works.

We cannot hope to achieve what is needed in the twenty-first century with our fragmented mix of disparate natural history institutions inherited from a past era. No matter how good our zoos might become, they are, by themselves and in their present form, inadequate to the tasks ahead. Some zoos have shown just how effective they can be in revealing the beauty and wonder of the world of animals. The bars have come down—now there are new barriers to overcome.

Rapunzel, an endangered female Sumatran rhino *(Dicerorhinus sumatrensis)* who is shown here at the Bronx Zoo but has since moved to Cincinnati, is part of the Sumatran Rhino Trust, directed by the Species Survival Plan. Responsible for monitoring breeding of the captive population of rhinos worldwide, the program has removed seven animals from the wild and placed them in various American zoos (San Diego, Cincinnati, Los Angeles, and the Bronx). But four rhinos have already died, putting the controversial program in jeopardy. Some biologists protest that the millions spent on this experiment should instead be directed toward preserving the natural habitat of the rhino.

At the Minnesota Zoo, veterinarian Chris Petrini and zookeepers Don Rasmussen and Jackie Fallon care for a newborn Bactrian camel *(Camelus bactrianus)*, while its anxious mother hovers behind. This is a postnatal checkup that every zoo baby receives—even one as enormous as this.

Torrey Pillsbury at the San Diego Wild Animal Park steers a young okapi *(Okapia johnstoni)* to safety during a flash thunderstorm. One of the park's rarest animals, the okapi is native to the humid forests of Zaire and was not even discovered until 1933.

Keeper Roẏ Riffe tosses fish to the sea lions *(Zalophus californianus)* on an icy February day at New York's Central Park Wildlife Center. Public feedings provide the animals with exercise and emotional contact and allow keepers to check their condition while they leap and preen.

At the Audubon Zoo in New Orleans, a white alligator floats while a keeper stands watch.

Over the years the dangers of handling elephants have become apparent, as many keepers have been injured or even killed. Handlers now emphasize the need for positive conditioning and the importance of work to prevent boredom in these intelligent beasts. At the National Zoo in Washington, D.C., elephants are washed daily and given periodic pedicures, allowing keepers to check the elephants' health and maintain relationships with the large and tremendously powerful animals.

A hissing, angry cougar *(Felis concolor)* prowls the Louisiana swamp exhibit at the Audubon Zoo. Of Rocky Mountain
origin, the cat is a stand-in for a severely endangered and rare subspecies, the Florida panther, which it resembles.

Future Fusion: The Twenty-First Century Zoo

Jon Charles Coe,
Landscape Architect, CLRdesign, Inc.

A giraffe and elephant cohabitate in the Africa exhibit at Pittsburgh Zoo.

Why are there zoos? Why do we wear fur coats, have potted plants and goldfish? Why do Americans have 60 million cats and 54 million dogs? Why do we admire butterflies, beauty bush, and birdsong? The answer is probably in our genes as well as our culture. Our pre-human primate ancestors lived or died by their ability to choose between nourishing and toxic plants, to detect the leopard in the grass and predict its actions. Keen, observant individuals had increased chances of passing on their genes.

Later, as hunter–gatherers for 90 percent of our human existence, people also survived (or didn't) largely because of their ability to identify and use beneficial plants and animals while avoiding dangerous ones. Those early ancestors not only appreciated utilitarian species but, if modern-day hunting–gathering societies are a measure, also appreciated the sublime sunset and the sacred mountain. Nature was appreciated at many levels.

The fact that you are reading these thoughts is sufficient proof that your ancestors, in an unbroken chain that stretches back to the beginning of life, were successful. While you may recognize the leopard in your cat, you may not make the connection between your carefully managed lawn and shade trees and your ancestral savanna home. Likewise, you may not relate your love of animals and visits to zoos with your previous life as a hunter–gatherer. But the same genetically based fascination with plants and animals explains the existence of zoos. This may explain why there are zoos, but to learn what they are like we must examine the history of zoos themselves.

Zoos have evolved with their times, yet their history opens a window on attitudes toward wildlife in different periods. Study shows that these attitudes were complex, and contradiction, then as now, was common. Nevertheless, two persistent lines of thought reach from ancient times to the present—two opposite philosophies that merge in zoos in our time. These are the evolution of zoos as displays of human power over nature *(homocentric)* and the evolution of animals as educational and ethical displays *(biocentric)*.

Recent zoo history began when the Machine Age of the Industrial Revolution spawned a new look at art and architecture that became known as the International Style. Forms became simple and severe, without ornament. In fact, Louis Sullivan's dictum that " . . . form must ever follow function" became the stylistic mandate. Implicit in this approach is the belief that research and technology, sufficiently applied, can fulfill all human (and animal) needs. This is the homocentric foundation of Modernism.

Zoos of the Modernist period from the 1950s to the 1970s in the United States took Carl Hagenbeck's naturalistic open-moated grottoes of 1907 and put them back into rows. Artificial rockwork, once grand and imposing, became abstracted. Nature was seen through gridded goggles, where animals were ordered by type: cat with cats, rhino with pachyderms. Even zoos that (such as Hagenbeck's Tierpark sixty years earlier) were organized around continental clusters (called "zoo-geographic arrangement") made little note of animal habitats.

Modernism also brought great improvements to zoos, especially in hygiene, veterinary care, and diet. This is the period of the blue-tile-lined, glass-fronted display area. Many species were setting longevity records, but relative to today, few were breeding. Wild animals were still trapped to stock zoos. In spite of the pioneering animal behavioral work of Heini Hedigar, Konrad Lorenz, and Robert Yerkes, the social needs of many species, essential to breeding, were largely overlooked.

With the late Modernist period came a tremendous upsurge in new zoo construction that might be called the Utopian period. Impatient with antiquated Victorian zoos in limited inner-city locations, some zoos believed their problems would be solved with "two hundred acres and a monorail." Zoos in Milwaukee, Toronto, Minneapolis, San Diego, and Miami moved to the suburbs. (The Indianapolis Zoo moved to a reclaimed site near the center of the city, but otherwise is included in this group). While the Utopian zoos can each point to important improvements, they all suffered badly from a misunderstanding of their primary audience—their faithful neighborhood visitors. People came from afar to see the grand new zoo, but repeat visitation was low. Caught up in the enormous effort of opening a new zoo, planners had exhausted all available resources—financial, leadership, and community support. There was simply nothing left for follow-up.

Planners had ignored what Hagenbeck understood—people came to the zoo as an attraction. Education and conservation are secondary concerns to the family planning their

A pygmy hippo *(Choeropsis liberiensis)*, extremely endangered in their fast-disappearing West African rainforest habitat, stands half-submerged at the Henry Doorly Zoo, Omaha.

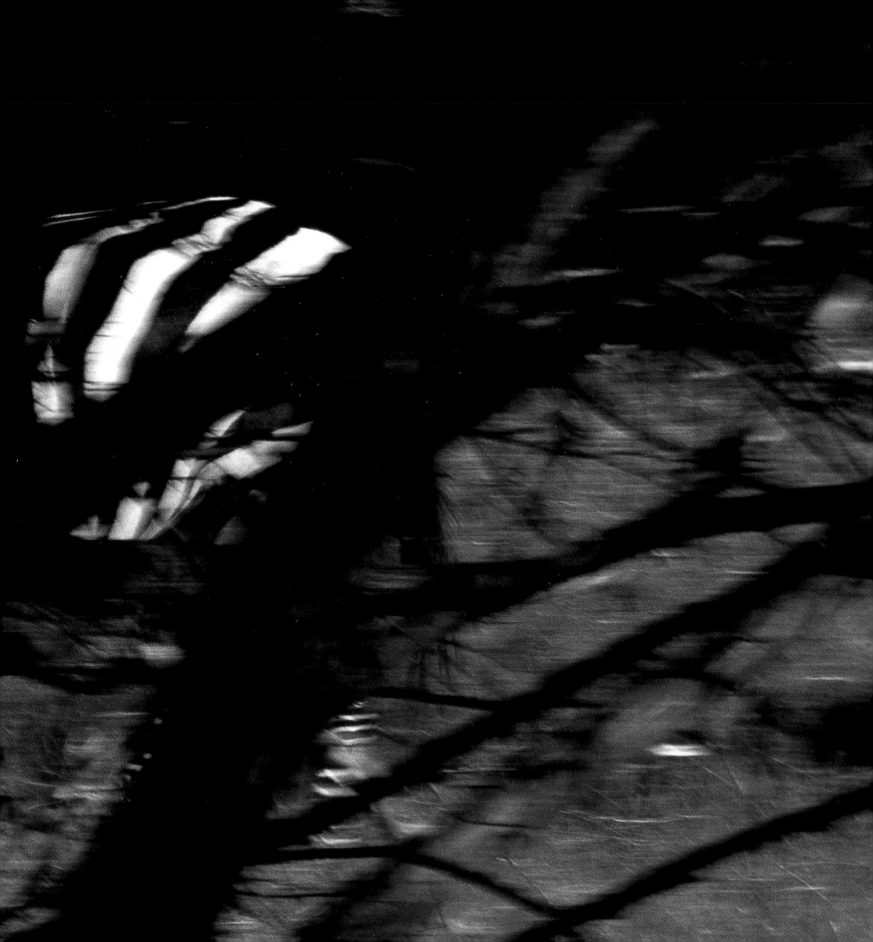

At the Asia exhibit at the Audubon Zoo in New Orleans, a black leopard *(Panthera pardus)* roams the jungle. More adaptable in the wild than other great cats, the leopard is increasingly suffering from loss of habitat. The color is actually a genetic accident—*panthera pardus* is not a separate species but simply a leopard without visible spots.

Preceding pages: A Grant's zebra *(Equus burchelli pamara)* browses on the grasslands at Fossil Rim, Texas, in an environment similar to that of its native African terrain.

ARIZONA-SONORA DESERT MUSEUM

2021 North Kinney Road
Tucson, AZ 85743
(602) 883-1380

The founders of the Desert Museum were clear that they didn't want a zoo, but rather a living museum, celebrating surrounding desert geology and plants as much as the native animals, and thus Arizona-Sonora became perhaps the first biopark. They also chose the most beautiful location a desert facility could ask for and proceeded to develop it with great ingenuity and respect—and that tradition continues to this day. The Earth Science Center begins as an adventure in caving through a breathtaking replication of passages in Carlsbad Caverns. The mountain trail among black bear, cougar, and wolf merges seamlessly with the surrounding desert, and the cat canyon and bighorn sheep exhibits were built well ahead of their time. The hummingbird aviary is popular because these winged jewels are so close and so numerous. Thanks to recent construction, visitor services are now first rate as well. The docent program, a strong point of most institutions on this list, is also excellent.

THE AUDUBON PARK AND
ZOOLOGICAL GARDEN

6500 Magazine Street
New Orleans, LA 70118
(504) 861-2537

Another rags-to-riches zoo tale resulted in a very popular zoo in a lovely old park. The Louisiana Swampland exhibit shows native animals and ecosystems beautifully. The Audubon Institute also built the new Aquarium of the Americas and sponsors valuable conservation research. Among zoo professionals, the Audubon Zoo is a model for business and fund-raising expertise.

BRONX ZOO/WILDLIFE CONSERVATION PARK

185th Street and Southern Boulevard
Bronx, NY 10460-1099
(718) 367-1010

Within the profession, the New York Zoological Society and its many facilities are internationally respected for their far-reaching field research and conservation programs (see William Conway's article in this volume). Not only is the collection vast, but many of the best and most beautiful exhibits yet designed are found here. These include JungleWorld (the progenitor of the Henry Doorly Zoo's rain forest exhibit); Himalayan Highlands (featuring the snow leopard); and Ethiopian Highlands (starring baboons and wild goats) with its splendid native village. The Zoo Court and the historic Elephant House represent the very best of the nineteenth-century zoo while World of Darkness, Wild Asia (with a monorail), and World of Birds (recently refurbished) were also international zoo trendsetters. There is also an outstanding education program, and the professional reputation of the staff is legendary.

BROOKFIELD ZOO/CHICAGO ZOOLOGICAL PARK

3300 Golf Road
Brookfield, IL 60513
(708) 485-0263

Suburban Chicago's spacious zoo with its European axes and beautiful gardens also has an excellent reputation for its many programs in support of international conservation. Popular features include Tropical World, a bold early entry into the indoor rain forest exhibit sweepstakes (where many species share voluminous habitats); Seven Seas Pavilion, a bright, attractive venue for a first-class marine mammal educational program; and Fragile Kingdom, a clever and often beautiful immersion exhibit featuring smaller animals. Habitat Africa! boasts a kopje within a kopje (a kopje is a large granite rock outcrop and the animals and plants that live there) and a water

hole. Featured animals include African hunting dogs, giraffe, antelope, and many fascinating and active small mammals, reptiles, and birds. This exhibit is especially celebrated for its innovative interpretive bush trail.

CALDWELL ZOO

2215 West Martin Luther King Boulevard
Tyler, TX 75702
(903) 593-0121

One of the four remaining North American zoos with free admission, the Caldwell Zoo, with more than 1,500 animals and 250 species, emphasizes three geographic regions: North America, South America, and East Africa. The East African Plains exhibit, the centerpiece of the zoo, won a special achievement award from the American Zoo and Aquarium Association. It features bongo antelope, elephants, crocodiles, African cyclids, leopards, and lions in an open-air, natural setting with artificial landscaping, where visitors can walk along shaded walkways, immersed in the landscape of the exhibit. The North American exhibit includes wild turkey, mountain lions, bobcats, and ocelots. Both of these sections include a fish and reptile house. The South American exhibit, the oldest section of the zoo (and slated for redevelopment), is based on an elongated flight cage containing both birds and animals. Species that are part of the exhibit include macaws, tapirs, squirrel monkeys, anteaters, and capybaras. Children will enjoy the petting area of the North American exhibit.

CENTRAL PARK WILDLIFE CENTER

East 64th Street and Fifth Avenue
New York, NY
(212) 861-6030

A few perverse New Yorkers still miss the old Central Park menagerie, but the new zoo is a proud heir to both the tradition and innovation of the New York Zoological Society, now the Wildlife

Conservation Society. It is an urban refuge of beauty and life, a delight to the senses. It is also a very effective fund-raising venue in the worthy cause of international wildlife conservation. Modeled upon the ancient Chinese "Garden of Intelligence," it fosters respect for nature through the enjoyment of seeing animals in beautiful settings in the context of a megalopolis.

CHEYENNE MOUNTAIN ZOO
4250 Cheyenne Mountain Zoo Road
Colorado Springs, CO 80906
(719) 633-0917

The only mountain zoo in the country, the Cheyenne Mountain Zoo is developing natural habitats for montaine animals. Built on the side of Cheyenne Mountain (by one of the founding fathers of Colorado Springs), the zoo's exhibits accessible by tram or walkway include Wolf Woods, which features three Mexican gray wolves, and Primate World, which features lowland gorillas, orangutans, a golden lion tamarind, and other primate species. In the Hidden Prairie exhibit, visitors can view the black-footed ferret, one of the most endangered American species that the zoo is involved in breeding, as well as the black-tailed prairie dog. The zoo is currently breaking ground on a project called Asian Highlands, which will eventually contain red pandas, Amur leopards, Siberian tigers, snow leopards, and black Asiatic bears.

CINCINNATI ZOO AND BOTANICAL GARDEN
3400 Vine Street
Cincinnati, OH 45220
(513) 281-4700

This zoo does everything very well and is an outstanding example of how a clear sense of mission can integrate and enliven a diverse institution. The horticultural program is widely respected in the profession and greatly admired by zoo visitors. The education programs delight thousands of children, and the research programs (the "frozen embryos zoo") are not only for scientists but are wonderfully accessible to the public. Cincinnati leads the nation with two groundbreaking exhibits: World of Insects and Butterfly Rainforest. It is again in the national zoo spotlight with its outdoor rain forest exhibit, Jungle Trail, featuring bonobos (pygmy chimpanzees) and other active primates.

COLUMBUS ZOO
9990 Riverside Drive
Powell, OH 43065
(614) 645-3400

The Columbus Zoo is perhaps best known for its popular Director-Emeritus, Jack Hanna, a nationally recognized TV personality and spokesperson for zoos. The zoo itself, which was the birthplace of the first captive-born gorilla back in 1956, is now home to one of the largest gorilla populations in the country. The cheetah population also has an impressive breeding track record, with 25 litters (88 cubs) born in just ten years, and recently the zoo has undertaken a strong program to breed the endangered red wolf. Buoyed by tremendous community support, the Columbus Zoo is a leader in expanding into alternative funding attractions, such as the adjacent golf course and amusement rides, both of which are owned and operated by the zoo and help support its conservation mission. In addition, the zoo was first to introduce overnight "zoo camps" (summer education programs designed for children) and offers an innovative training program for teachers.

FORT WORTH ZOO
1989 Colonial Parkway
Fort Worth, TX 76110
(817) 871-7050

The Fort Worth Zoo was best known for its reptile collection. But with privatization, the Fort Worth Zoo made a commitment not only to major new exhibits, but also to becoming extremely visitor-friendly. This head-to-toe cleanup and makeover, together with the new attractions, a great ape facility, an African savanna, and a dramatic tiger canyon/waterfall, have given the zoo a remarkable rebirth. Other zoos needing a turnaround should visit Fort Worth.

THE HENRY DOORLY ZOO
3701 South Tenth Street
Omaha, NE 68107-2200
(402) 733-8401

In the contest to build indoor rain forest exhibits, the Lied Jungle at Henry Doorly is certainly the biggest, and, from the visitor's point of view, it is breathtaking. Where else can you be buzzed by large fruit bats or walk on the spongy soil of the forest itself, among giant buttress trees, beautiful birds, and giant tapirs? Even experienced jungle trekkers will be delighted. Other equally wonderful exhibits are coming soon, including a large aquarium.

LINCOLN PARK ZOO
2200 North Cannon Drive
Chicago, IL 60614
(312) 294-4660

This midtown Chicago zoo has done a great deal in a very small site—even managing to birth and raise a baby elephant. Nearing the completion of one of the nation's most effective and sustained capital campaigns, the Lincoln Park Zoo continues to recreate itself, combining renovations of historic architecture with modern buildings buried underground. The Fisher Great Ape House features one of the largest collections anywhere, largely because of an outstanding breeding program. The innovative Regenstein Small Mammal Reptile House is soon to open.

MINNESOTA ZOO

13000 Zoo Boulevard
Apple Valley, MN 55124-8199
(612) 432-9000

Built along the lines of a modern Utopian zoo, with hundreds of acres, a monorail, and a mega-structure space to house tropical animals and plants, the Minnesota Zoo opened in the mid-1970s. Yet it is the rolling hills and winter ski trail to the Siberian tiger exhibit that strike the visitor. In today's age of habitat immersion, the massive concrete structures seem hard-edged and intrusive, but the Minnesota Zoo nevertheless broke important ground and remains very popular. Recent renovations have improved conditions for animals and renewed community interest. Breeding programs for tigers and other species and the scientific pedigree programs that originated at the Minnesota Zoo are greatly appreciated by zoo professionals. The Adopt-A-Park programs, through which American zoos support national parks in Third-World countries, originated here.

THE NATIONAL ZOOLOGICAL PARK

3001 Connecticut Avenue, NW
Washington, DC 20008
(202) 673-4821 or (202) 673-4717

The National Zoo has long been respected for its professional expertise; its animal collections, including unusual animals such as the giant panda; its education programs; and its support of international conservation efforts such as the golden lion tamarin release program. In the last few years, the creation of Olmsted Walk added greatly to the beauty of the grounds. Most recently, the exhibit Amazonia, with its splendid underwater walk along a river, hands-on discovery opportunity in a simulated research camp, and stroll through an indoor rain forest, brought the zoo into the age of highly naturalistic exhibits.

What makes Amazonia unique is that the titi monkeys in the trees above are not confined. Many complain that they don't see the animals, but the patient (or fortunate) get a real treat when the monkeys do appear.

NORTH CAROLINA ZOOLOGICAL PARK

4401 Zoo Parkway
Asheboro, NC 27203-9416

The North Carolina Zoo is big, and facilities are wildly dispersed among the boulders and forests sloping up to Purgatory Mountain. The African exhibits are very large—it's wonderful to see elephants in a sea of green—and the blending of natural geology and artificial rockwork appears seamless. New North American exhibits include a large, exciting polar bear area, a desert dome, a swamp, and other state-of-the-art exhibits. The Reynolds Forest Aviary, which is a geodesic dome, is especially beautiful.

NORTHWEST TREK WILDLIFE PARK

11610 Trek Drive, E
Eatonville, WA 98328
(206)832-6116

This 600-acre facility perched on the slopes of Mt. Rainier is to the Pacific Northwest what the Arizona-Sonora Desert Museum is to the Southwest. The natural site is fabulous, the exhibits understated, and the human interventions into the landscape are respectfully accomplished. Narrated tram tours take visitors among free-ranging bison, elk, mountain goat, bighorn sheep, moose, and other native species, making it a photographer's delight. Large bear and wolf exhibits are also noteworthy.

PITTSBURGH ZOO

1 Hill Road
Pittsburgh, PA 15206-1178
(412) 665-3639

This relatively unknown and underappreciated zoo transformed itself from one of the worst zoos in the nation to one of the best by eliminating the old barred cages and displaying animals in large immersion exhibits. The Siberian tiger and African savanna exhibits are excellent early examples of immersion exhibits with mature vegetation.

POINT DEFIANCE ZOO AND AQUARIUM

5400 North Pearl Sreet
Tacoma, WA 98407
(206) 591-5337

Located on a beautiful rise of land above Puget Sound, this small zoo is often overlooked. But those who do visit it are amazed by the beauty of the natural habitat exhibits—especially those for polar bear (perhaps the best yet built), musk ox, seals, walrus, and sea otter—as well as the Coral Reef exhibit in the Aquarium.

RIVERBANKS ZOOLOGICAL PARK & BOTANICAL GARDENS

500 Wildlife Parkway
P.O. Box 1060
Columbia, SC 29202-1060
(803) 977-8730 or (803) 779-8717

This is a small, friendly zoo with some world-class surprises, such as the Aquarium Reptile Complex, and innovative displays of reptiles, amphibians, and fish organized around habitat themes (some local, some international). Visitors can experience a Carolina swamp, a Southwest desert, an Asian rain forest, and a coral reef. The upgraded African savanna exhibit shows what excellent results can be obtained with a modest outlay of cash and truckloads of creativity.

The new botanical garden across the river includes several rare and beautiful native plants and is a delight for bird-watchers.

SAN DIEGO WILD ANIMAL PARK
15500 San Pasqual Valley Road
Escondido, CA 92027-7017
(619) 747-8702

This vast zoo, set in a warm, mild climate much like that of East Africa, was designed to become a world leader in breeding tropical and subtropical animals, and it has not disappointed. The park remains a trendsetter, with its beautiful plantings (started from scratch) and its visitor-friendly shops and services. New exhibits such as the butterfly aviaries are now beginning to provide the attendance revenue the park needs to really show what can be done there. Expect to see some major innovations in the next decade.

SAN DIEGO ZOO
P.O. Box 551
San Diego, CA 92112

The world-renowned San Diego Zoo had coasted on its reputation and multimillion-dollar advertising campaign for a long time. In the last decade, however, it has been rebuilding at a furious pace. Many of the new exhibits are outstanding, blessed by horticultural opportunities and expertise that are the envy of the nation. San Diego is also justly famous for its contributions to research. The traditional strengths in food and gift sales, and a theme-parklike devotion to entertainment and marketing, once scorned by "proper zoological parks," now serve as models for facilities eager to thrive in a world of declining public subsidies. Zoos across the nation, caught up in the rush toward privatization, look to the San Diego Zoo, which has always been financially self-sufficient, for inspiration.

ST. LOUIS ZOO
Forest Park
St. Louis, MO 63110
(314) 781-0900

This big, parklike facility appears (at first) to be the very model of the "traditional zoo." Yet St. Louis has always been a groundbreaker, beginning with its 1904 World's Fair aviary and its 1917 open-moated bear grottoes. During the 1970s the traditional Primate, Bird, and Reptile houses were attractively remodeled. Living World may be *the* exhibit of the '90s, a multimedia electronic learning center that has zoo professionals divided. Some see this ambitious project as a precursor of the virtual-reality zoo of tomorrow, perfect for today's computer-friendly kids; others argue that overkill simulation and computer obsolescence will make it an electronic relic. Since the experts can't agree, you should see it and decide for yourself.

TOLEDO ZOO
2700 Broadway
Toledo, OH 43609
(419) 385-5721

Toledo is the "little zoo that could" and did turn itself around from nearly closing down to becoming perhaps the most popular zoo for its size in the country. Groundbreaking exhibits include the African Savanna, with its Hippoquarium, where visitors can enjoy the surprising grace of these huge creatures, and the renovated Great Ape House, a model for animal behavioral enrichment and close-up viewing. The Diversity of Life learning center is a favorite of educators around the world, and the old WPA-built Museum, Theater, and Aquarium are still remarkable. In fact, the historic zoo architecture at the Toledo Zoo is worth a visit in itself, offering a creative response to the question of how to convert historic buildings to modern facilities. Toledo converted the old Carnivore House into the Carnivore Café, where patrons dine in repainted cages.

WOODLAND PARK ZOO
5500 Phinney Avenue, N
Seattle, WA 98103
(206) 684-4800

The Woodland Park Zoo was one of the founders of the landscape or habitat immersion exhibits that are now state of the art across the nation. The African Savanna, gorilla, and other exhibits influenced later exhibits in San Diego, Toledo, Pittsburgh, Atlanta, New York, and elsewhere, yet they remain both beautiful and functional in their own right. Newer award-winning exhibits include the Thai Elephant Forest and the Rain Forest, each a trendsetter. Seattle's newest award candidate is Northern Trail. Regarded by amateurs and professionals alike as one of the most beautiful natural habitat exhibits, it features a walk-through Alaska, with wolf, elk, Kodiak bear, otters, mountain goats, and eagles. Woodland Park also has an outstanding education and docent program and shows that a city-run zoo can be first class.

ZOO ATLANTA
800 Cherokee Avenue, SE
Atlanta, GA 30315
(404) 624-5600

Not long ago the Atlanta Zoo was considered one of America's ten worst. In reversing its name and fortunes, Zoo Atlanta became an inspiration to many other zoos on the hard road to revitalization. Atlanta's favorite silverback gorilla, Willie B, lived indoors by himself for twenty-seven years. Now he lives in a gorilla troop and has sired offspring. Willie lives with nineteen other gorillas in the Ford African Rainforest, one of the most naturalistic and innovative great ape exhibits anywhere. Recently Atlanta's gorillas were joined by an impressive silverback named Ivan, himself recently rescued from an isolated existence in a shopping center. Zoo Atlanta also has trendsetting immersion exhibits, an excellent reptile collection, and an outstanding education program.

BIBLIOGRAPHY

Batten, Peter. *Living Trophies*. New York: Thomas Y. Crowell Co., 1976. Considers purposes of zoos; animal dealers' breeding programs; animal husbandry, notes, and index.

Bendiner, Robert. *The Fall of the Wild, the Rise of the Zoo*. New York: E.P. Dutton, 1981. Article on zoos and evolution of the zoo.

Benyus, Janine. *Beastly Behaviors*. Reading, Mass.: Addison Wesley, 1992. What makes cranes dance, whales whistle, and crocodiles roar; informative about animal behavior.

Blunt, Wilfrid. *The Ark in the Park: The Zoo in the Nineteenth Century*. London: Hamish Hamilton Ltd., 1976. A well-illustrated history of the Zoological Society of London, the model from which the modern zoo emerged.

Bostock, Stephen. *Zoos and Animal Rights*. London: Routledge, 1993. Discusses the ethics of keeping animals in zoos; argues that zoos have a conservation role.

Briere, Alan and Steve Dale. *American Zoos*. New York: Mallard Press, 1992. An illustrated book on zoos.

Bridges, William. *Gathering of Animals, An Unconventional History of the New York Zoological Society*. New York: Harper & Row, 1966. Fascinating account of the people and events leading to the creation of one of the world's great zoological enterprises.

Bruns, Bill. *A World of Animals: The San Diego Zoo and the Wild Animal Park*. New York: Abrams, 1983.

Campbell, Sheldon. *Lifeboats to Ararat*. New York: Times Books, 1978. Addresses the mission of zoos in saving rare and endangered species.

Cherfas, Jeremy. *Zoo 2000: a Look Beyond the Bars*. London, BBC, 1984. The new zoo examined.

Cohen, Daniel and Susan Cohen. *Zoos*. New York: Doubleday, 1992. A children's book.

Curtis, Lawrence. *Zoological Park Fundamentals*. Washington, D.C.: National Recreation and Park Association, 1968. Outdated but interesting booklet on zoo planning and design.

Durrell, Gerald. *The Ark's Anniversary*. New York: Arcade Publishing, 1990. A look at the Jersey Wildlife Preservation Trust, on the occasion of its anniversary.

_____. *State of the Ark*. New York: Doubleday, 1986.

_____. *The Stationary Ark*. London: Collins, 1976.

Fisher, James. *Zoos of the World: The Story of Animals in Captivity*. New York: Natural History Press, 1967. An excellent account of the history of zoos from the Pharaohs to the 1960s.

Gold, Don. *Zoo: A Behind-the-Scenes Look at the Animals and the People Who Care for Them*. Chicago: Contemporary Books, 1988.

Hagenbeck, Carl. *Beasts and Men, Being Carl Hagenbeck's Experiences for Half a Century Among Wild Animals* (abridged and translated by Hugh S.R. Elliot and Arthur Gordon Thacker). London: Longmans, Green and Company, 1909. Fascinating biography of one of the most innovative zoo thinkers and doers of all time.

Hahn, Emily. *Animal Gardens, or Zoos Around the World*. London: Begos & Rosenberg, Inc., 1967, 1990. Personal journeys to zoos, based on the original *The New Yorker* articles.

Hancocks, David. *Animals and Architecture*. New York: Praeger, 1971. A comprehensive review of zoo history and a worldwide survey of zoo design and planning.

Hanna, Jack. *Monkeys on the Interstate and Other Tales from America's Favorite Zookeeper*. New York: Doubleday, 1989.

Hediger, Heini. *Man and Animal in the Zoo*. New York: Delacorte, 1969. Considers three key factors in the management of animals in zoos: living space, diet, and animal–human relationships.

_____. *The Psychology and Behavior of Animals in Zoos and Circuses*. New York: Dover Publications, Inc., 1968. Essential reading for anyone involved in designing for animals in captivity.

_____. *Wild Animals in Captivity*. New York: Dover Publications, Inc. 1964. Modern methods of keeping rare wild animals, by a famous zoological park director.

Hutchins, Mike, et al. eds. *Ethics on the Ark*. Washington, D.C.: Smithsonian Institution Press, 1995. A provocative and thoughtful series of essays on the dilemmas of zoos, animal welfare, and wildlife conservation.

Huxley, Elspeth. *Whipsnade: Captive Breeding for Survival*. London: Collins, 1981.

Jenkins, C.F. *The Noah's Ark Syndrome*. Sydney, Australia: Zoological Gardens Board of Western Australia, 1977. Review of 100 years of zoo development in Australia.

Kleiman, D. M. Allen, K. Thompson, eds. *Wild Mammals in Captivity*. Chicago: University of Chicago Press, 1995. In-depth essays on basic husbandry, nutrition, exhibitors, population management, behavior, reproduction, and research.

Koebner, Linda. *Zoo: The Evolution of Wildlife Conservation Parks*. New York: Tom Doherty Associates, Inc., 1994. A coffee-table book all about the purposes, practices, and people who make zoos what they are and what they can become.

Luoma, R. Jon, *A Crowded Ark*. Boston: Houghton Miffin, 1987. Examines the scientific, political, and social issues surrounding zoos.

Maier, Franz and Jake Page. *Zoo: The Modern Ark*. New York: Facts on File, 1990. A general introduction to zoos, heavily illustrated.

Maple, Terry. and Erika F. Archibald. *Zoo Man: Inside the Zoo Revolution*. Atlanta: Longstreet Press, 1993. Chronicles the transformation of the Atlanta Zoo as a window into the international revolution in zoo design and philosophy.

Martin, R. D., ed. *Breeding Endangered Species in Captivity*. London/New York: Academic Press, 1975. Forty different contributors with articles on the breeding of various species in captivity.

Mullan, Bob, and Garry Marvin. *Zoo Culture*. London: Weidenfeld and Nicolson, 1987. A worldwide survey of zoos, zookeepers, and especially zoogoers, focusing on the cultural phenomenon of zoos.

Olney, P., ed. *International Zoo Yearbook*. London: Zoological Society of London. Annual publication in production since 1959 dealing with all aspects of zoo operations, husbandry, breeding, exhibits. An invaluable resource.

O'Neill, Michael. *Zoobabies*. New York: Abrams, 1993. A children's book.

Peterson, Dale. *The Deluge and the Ark: A Journey into Private Worlds*. Boston: Houghton Mifflin, 1989. The role of zoos in primate conservation.

Rinard, Judith. *Zoos Without Cages*. Washington, D.C.: National Geographic Society, 1981.

Sausman, Karen, (ed.). *Zoological Park and Aquarium Fundamentals*. Wheeling, W.Va.: American Association of Zoological Parks and Aquariums, 1982. Discussion of conservation design.

Sedgewick, John. *The Peaceable Kingdom: A Year in the Life of America's Oldest Zoo*. New York: William Morrow, 1988. A readable account of the Philadelphia Zoo.

Tudge, Colin. *Last Animals at the Zoo: How Mass Extinction Might Be Stopped*. London: Hutchinson Radius, 1991. A fascinating and provocative account.

Ulmer, Jefferson G. and Susan Gower. *Lions and Tigers and Bears: A Guide to Zoological Parks*. New York: Garland, 1985. State-by-state guide to zoos, visitor centers, nature centers, and marine life displays in the United States and Canada.

Virtue, Noel. *Among the Animals: a zookeeper's story*. London: Peter Owen, 1988. A readable account from a keeper at the London Zoo.

_____. *Why Zoos?* UFAW Courier No 24. London: Universities Federation for Animal Welfare, 1988. Short collection of essays discussing the function of zoos.

Zuckerman, Solly. *Great Zoos of the World: Their Origins and Significance*. London: Weidenfeld and Nicholson, 1980.

INDEX

Bold entries are for photographic pages.

Published by Thomasson-Grant & Lickle

Copyright © 1996 Lickle Publishing .

Photographs and Introduction © 1996 Michael Nichols.

Essays © 1996 by (in order of appearance):

William Conway, Michael H. Robinson,

Edward J. Maruska, Jack Hanna, David Hancocks,

Jon Charles Coe.

Editor: Nan Richardson, Umbra Editions, New York.

Art Direction: Lisa Lytton-Smith.

Inquiries should be directed to:

Thomasson-Grant & Lickle

106 South Street

Charlottesville, Virginia 22902

(804) 977-1780

Printed in Hong Kong

00 99 98 97 96 95   5 4 3 2 1

Library of Congress
Cataloging-in-Publication Data

Nichols, Michael.
    Keepers of the kingdom : the new American zoo / photographs by
  Michael Nichols ; essays by Jon Coe . . . [et al.].
        p. cm.
    Includes bibliographical references (p.   ) and index.
    ISBN 0-9650308-2-2 (hard). -- ISBN 0-9650308-3-0 (soft)
    1. Zoos--United States. 2. Zoos--United States--Pictorial works.
  I. Coe, Jon Charles. II. Title.
    QL76.5.U6N535 1995
    590' .74'473--dc20   95-23922
                                                        CIP